Picking Apples

by

Gail Saunders-Smith

Pebble Books

an imprint of Capstone Press

Library Media Center
G. Brooks Elementary School
2700 Stonebridge Blvd.
Aurora, IL 60504

1

Pebble Books

Pebble Books are published by Capstone Press
818 North Willow Street, Mankato, Minnesota 56001
http://www.capstone-press.com
Copyright © 1998 by Capstone Press

All Rights Reserved • Printed in the United States of America

Library of Congress Cataloging-in-Publication Data
Saunders-Smith, Gail.
  Picking apples/by Gail Saunders-Smith.
    p. cm.
  Includes bibliographical references (p. 23) and index.
  Summary: Simple text and photographs describe the process
of getting apples from the tree to trucks that are used to ship
them everywhere.
  ISBN 1-56065-585-2
  1. Apples--Harvesting--Juvenile literature. [1. Apples--
Harvesting.] I. Title.

SB363.35.S38 1998
634'.115--dc21   97-29797
                                           CIP
                                            AC

Editorial Credits
Lois Wallentine, editor; Timothy Halldin and James Franklin,
design; Michelle L. Norstad, photo research

Photo Credits
John Marshall Outdoor Photography, 1, 4, 6, 18, 20
Mark Turner, 10, 12, 16
Unicorn Stock/Alice Prescott, 8; Martha McBride, 14
Valan Photos/Charlene Daley, cover

2

Table of Contents

Apple pickers use special bags.

Sometimes they use ladders.

Sometimes they
use special poles.

They lift and twist
the apples off.

They put the apples in their bags.

They empty their bags into bins.

They lift the bins with tractors.

They load the bins on trucks.

Trucks take the
apples everywhere.

Words to Know

apple pickers—people who pick apples from trees

bins—large boxes that hold apples

ladder—a tool people use to climb up and down; it is usually made out of wood, metal, or rope

special bag—a large bag that an apple picker uses to carry apples; the bag has stiff sides with a long, cloth bag attached that can open at the bottom

special pole—a long pole that an apple picker uses to reach up into a tree and pick an apple; the pole has a small, wire basket on the end

22

Read More

Burckhardt, Ann L. *Apples.* Mankato, Minn.: Bridgestone Books, 1996.

Hutchings, Amy and Richard Hutchings. *Picking Apples and Pumpkins.* New York: Scholastic, Inc., 1994.

Micucci, Charles. *The Life and Times of the Apple.* New York: Orchard Books, 1992.

Internet Sites

Neva's Apple Page
http://www.tcgcs.com/~nrolls/apples.html

Talk About Apples
http://www.tossed-salad.com/apple.html

Washington Apple Commission Home Page
http://www.bestapples.com

Note to Parents and Teachers

This book illustrates and describes the process of picking apples. The clear photographs support the beginning reader in making and maintaining the meaning of the text. Children may need assistance in using the Table of Contents, Words to Know, Read More, Internet Sites, and Index/Word List sections of the book.

Index/Word List

Word Count: 51